Published in the United States of America

Brilliant Books Literary
137 Forest Park Lane Thomasville
North Carolina 27360 USA

ISBN:
Paperback: 979-8-88945-506-6
Ebook: 979-8-88945-507-3

INTRODUCTION

Hello, my name is Virgil Revish, is an author, consultant, speaker and mentor. I taught at Junior High until I joined the U.S Army and served for 3 to 6 years. Due to my devotion to students and education, I returned to teaching. I taught in Fairfax, Va. for years. Later I worked at Petersburg Wastewater Treatment Plant, testing water samples and reading meters. From September 1995 to June 1999. I started a volunteer program called "School Watch" in Six Petersburg School.

In 2000. I worked in an after school program called "Achievers Plus at the Children's Home of Virginia Baptist. I continued to pursue opportunities to serve students and the community. I worked with other visionaries and committed community leaders to encourage the youth. I am also the "Associate Producer" of "Pull Your Pants Up" project and video, a nationwide initiative designed to encourage the youth to be responsible, accountable and prepared to meet and exceed the acceptable societal standards and rise above the norm.

I. In the <u>first</u> chapter, I will talk about "<u>School Watch</u>". September 1994-June 1999

II. Chapter 2 – How Vision: Going To The Next Level

<u>Program Prepare for College</u>
   a) Pre- High School
   b) Do your best in School
   c) Become involved in School Community
   d) Go to Career information events.

III. <u>Chapter 3</u> – Putting Plan in Place, if wanted to go to D1 Program

IV. <u>Chapter 4</u> –Upton Bailey Success

V. Accomplishment From Program:
Vision: Going To The Next Level, Virgil Revish

I Like To Dedicate My Book
To My Mother & Father,

Mr. & Mrs. Willie & Viola Revish

CHAPTER #1

SCHOOL WATCH

"SCHOOL WATCH"

From September 1994 to June 1999, I started a Volunteer Program called "School Watch", which was in six Petersburg Public Schools. Mr. Larry Brown asked me, would I be interested in this volunteer program, "School Watch". I told him I would look over the material. The material contain, the object and intent. I got back with Mr. Brown, and I told him that I was interested. We were supported by the Petersburg High School Boosters Club. This is "School Watch" – Logo: Protecting the Pathway to success. Established October 3, 1994-1999.

CONGRATULATIONS!!!

School Watch Volunteer/Supporter

Object and Intent

"School Watch" is an organized and well-coordinated group of volunteer school supporters such as parents, retirees, alumnus, and staff, who pledge to provide visual and psychological security on as needed basis, to the school system. In addition, they will coordinate activities along with support groups of the school to provide assistance for extracurricular activities and projects to keep adults from being truant and from dropping out of school.

MISSION

Our mission is to:
- Assist in creating a safe, secure and nurturing environment which encourage our young adults to become responsible citizens.
- Develop a strong and effective working partnership with school officials.
- Assist in the learning and extracurricular opportunities for students and encouraging positive activities to keep students off the streets and in school.
- Provide role model for young adults.

Definitions:

School Watch Volunteers – Provide service on a schedule or on call basis for a.m. and p.m. school functions, ie., hall monitor, field trips, help in classrooms, evening activities, etc.

School Watch Supporter – Not on a schedule, or on call basis, however, they have pledged to support school watch by wearing their name tag when normally attending school events, sporting events, assemblies, etc. They will be seated throughout the crowd for visual and psychological effect.

School Watch Assignments & Duties

- Assist with school safety and security via monitoring assigned areas, i.e., halls, cafeteria, parking lots, social events, etc.
- Chaperon on field trips
- Guest speakers
- Role Model
- Mentor
- Tutors.

Handling Serious Behaviours or Discipline Problem

Steps to take:

1. If a School Watch Volunteer/ Supporter observes two or more students in a physical conflict or verbal altercation, do not physically intervene.
2. Get help from a teacher, Administrator or Police Officer
3. Assist other staff members by asking students to move away from the situation.
4. If possible, provide any information that will be helpful in determining the cause of the altercation to a teacher, the School Administrator or Police Officer.

Training – All volunteers/supporters must attend an orientation session to be held by school administration personnel or the Police Department. For information: Virgil Revish: virgilrevishi@yahoo.com

Congratulations!!!

School/ Watch Organizations Established 1994-1999

Petersburg High School

Peabody Middle School

Walnut Hill Elementary

These are the "School Watch" Jackets that the Petersburg High School Boosters Club donated money for the "School Watch Jackets".

Pictures of Jackets of "<u>School Watch</u>"!

School Watch

Certificate of Appreciation
presented to Virgil Revish
1997 "School Watch"
Certificate of Appreciation
Petersburg High School-Booster Club

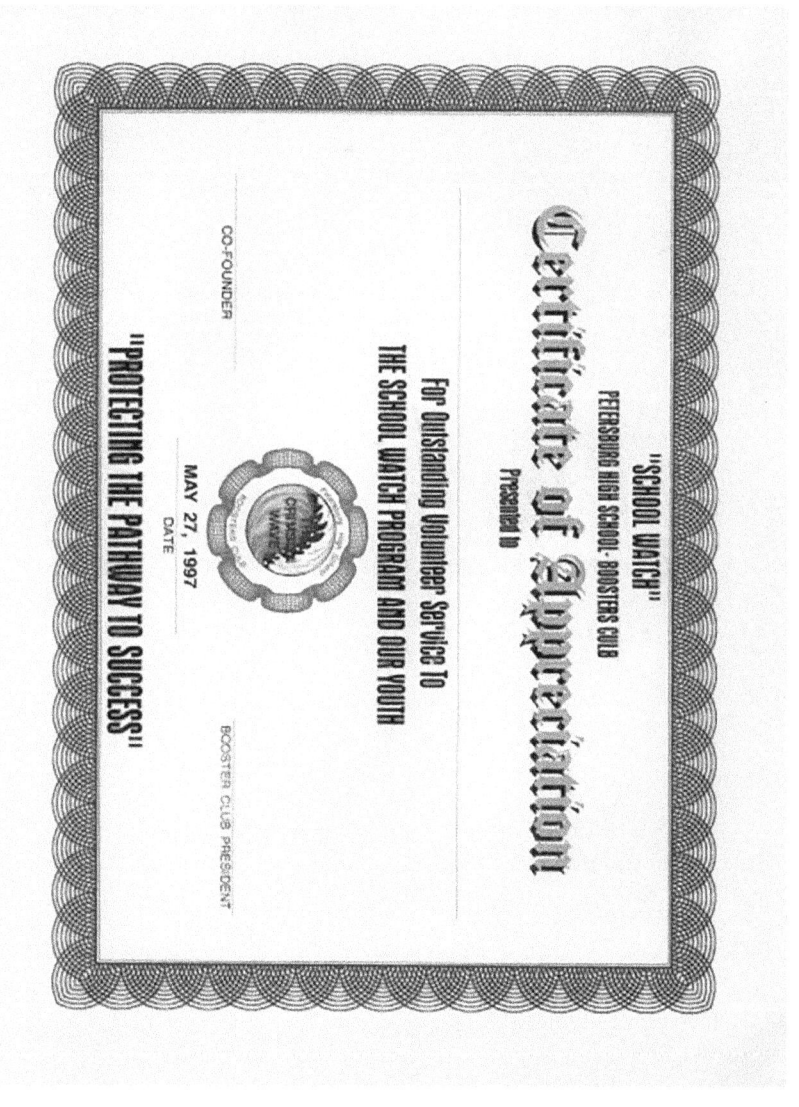

COMMONWEALTH of VIRGINIA

Office of the Governor
August 14, 1998

James S. Gilmore,III   Gary K. Aronhalt
Governor   Secretary of Public Safety

Mr. Virgil Revish
Area Coordinator
School Watch Volunteer Program
Post Office Box 573
Petersburg, Virginia 23803

Dear Mr. Revish:

The Governor has asked me to thank you for and respond to your letter expressing how the School Watch Volunteer Program has been successful in some of the Petersburg area schools.

I would like to commend your efforts and those of the other volunteers for recognizing and taking action in your local school system. Governor James Gilmore shares your views concerning protecting our youth and thus has proposed a 21-point plan to address public safety and crime prevention issues. The New Partnership Commission is the first point in that plan. Violence, in our schools and elsewhere, presents a clear danger to our children and our families. No one program and no one community can stand alone against this danger. The Commission will unite our citizens, our communities and our corporations to combat violence and promote safety throughout the Commonwealth.

The Commission will be holding meetings across Virginia in the coming months. They will look to community leaders and interested citizens for recommendations and assistance. The Commission members will be made aware of your interest and experience. I hope that your organization and others around the state will bring together new ideas and initiatives to promote positive opportunities for our youth. We look forward to working with you on this important issue.

Again, thank you for your letter, and I commend you for your efforts.

Sincerely,

Gary K. Aronhalt

GKA/krw

P.O. Box 1475 · Richmond, Virginia 23218 ·
(804) 786-5351 · TDD (804) 786-7765

School Watch

September 11, 1999, Ms. Barbara Brown, Principal of Petersburg High School would like for Petersburg High School to be the first School in the nation to erect a School Watch sign in front of the school.

SCHOOL WATCH   PETERSBURG PUBLIC SCHOOLS

September 11, 1999

BARBARA BROWN
PRINCIPAL, PETERSBURG HIGH SCHOOL
PETERSBURG, VIRGINIA

DEAR MRS. BROWN:

THE SCHOOL WATCH PROGRAM WOULD LIKE FOR
PETERSBURG HIGH SCHOOL TO BE THE FIRST SCHOOL
IN THE NATION TO ERECT A SCHOOL WATCH SIGH
IN FRONT OF THE SCHOOL..SCHOOL SAFETY IS A
NATIONWIDE CONCERN; THEREFORE, WE WOULD
LIKE TO CONTINUE TO DEMONSTRATE LEADERSHIP IN
ADDRESSING THIS CONCERN.

THE SCHOOL WATCH PROGRAM WAS ESTABLISHED AT
PETERSBURG HIGH SCHOOL ON OCTOBER 3, 1994. OUR
VOLUNTEERS ARE COMMITTED TO PROTECTING THE
PATHWAY TO SUCCESS FOR ALL STUDENTS. WE BELIEVE,
ERECTING A SCHOOL WATCH SIGH ALONG WITH
TRAINING VOLUNTEERS, ADMINISTRATORS, STAFF, AND
STUDENTS TO OBSERVE AND REPORT CRIME, WOULD
SET AN EXAMPLE FOR OTHER SCHOOLS TO FOLLOW
THROUGHOUT THE NATION.

THANKS IN ADVANCE FOR YOUR CONSIDERATION OF
OUR REQUEST.

SINCERELY,

Virgil Revish

VIRGIL REVISH,
AREA COORDINATOR FOR SCHOOL WATCH

CC: COFOUNDERS:
YEVETTE ROBINSON
ALFRED GOODE
LARRY BROWN, SR.
VANESSA CRAWFORD (PHS BOOSTERS CLUB
3/7/23, 2:24 PM   (37,845 unread) – virgilrevish@yahoo.com –
Yahoo Mail

How vision: Going To The Next Level, Program (1)Preparing for college Introduction:

2

COLLEGE PREPARATION CHECKLIST

9th Grade

- Pre-High School. Start saving for college. If you haven't already. Look into college savings Plans that your state may offer.

- Do your best in school. If you are having difficulty, don't give up; get help from a teacher, tutor or mentor.

- Become involved in school or community based extra-curricular activities that enable you to explore your interest, meet new people and learn new things.

- Go to career information events. Ask employees to have next.

- Meet with your school counselor or mentor to discuss college and their requirements.

High School Every Year

- Continue to Save for College

- Take Challenging classes in core academic subjects most colleges require four years of English , at least three years of social studies (history, civic, geography, economic, etc) three years of mathematics, and 2 years of a foreign language. Round out Your Core load with classes in Computer science and the Arts.

Stay involved in School or Community based extra-curricular activities that interest you or enable you to explore career interest. Consider working or volunteering. Remember, its quality (not quantity that counts).

- Talk to Your School Counselor and other mentor about education after high school. Your Counsel can answer questions about what classes to take on high school.

9th Grade Core Curriculum

a) English 9th
b) Math (algebra1, or Geometry or algebra2)
c) Science (Biology, or Earth Science)
d) Social Studies (US, History)
e) General Electives (Fine Arts, Music Technology/ Computer Science, Physical Education)
f) Foreign Language (Spanish, French)

10th Grade –Register with the NCAA Eligibility Center.Org

Division 1- Academic Eligibility-

To be eligible to compete in NCAA Sports during your first year at a Division1 School, you must graduate high school and meet all the following requirements:
- Complete 16 Core Courses
- Four years of English
- Three years of Math (algebra, or higher)
- Two years of Natural/Physical Science (including one year of lab science if your high school offer it.)

10th Grade Core Curriculum
a. English 10th Grade
b. Math (Geometry ,or Algebra2 or Pre-calculus)
c. Science (Chemistry)
d. Social Studies (American Government)

11th Grade – Continue to Challenge yourself academically.
- Research Colleges That interest you
- Investigate financial aid , including Scholarships
- Understand the different types and sources of aid.
- For more information about scholarships and federal student aid opportunities. Visit: wwwfederalair.ed.gov.
- Make sure you have completed your SOl by the 11th grade.

10th Fall- Take the preliminary SAT/National
- Merit Scholarship Qualifying Test (PSAT/NMSQT). You must take the test in the 11th grade to qualify for scholarships and Programs associated with the National Merit program.

Summer Before 12th Grade

- Narrow down the list of colleges you are interested in attending. If you can, visit the school that interest you.

- Contact colleges to request information and applications for admission. Ask about financial aid, admission requirement and deadlines.

- Decide whether you are going to apply under a particular College's early decision or early action program. Be sure to learn about program deadlines and requirements.

*Remember: Register for all test, in advance and be sure to give yourself time to prepare appropriately! If you have difficulty paying a registration fee, see your school counsellor about getting fee waiver.

COLLEGE BOUND

1. **<u>Get your child involved</u>**: One you're thinking that your child's future includes college, you can help him/her believe it too. Get a big envelope to keep all of his/her records of classes and extracurricular activities.

    *   <u>Talk to the teachers:</u> Make a point of meeting with teachers every year; they are your partners in helping your Child to succeed. Include your child's concerns too.

    *   <u>Be sure the Core Curriculum is covered:</u> Your child should start with no fewer than five solid academic classes per semester. Standard courses for College Success include this core curriculum for grade 9, through 12:

<u>English-</u> (writing; literature) :	4 years
<u>Math-</u> (geometry; algebra;	
and advanced math include algebra II:	4 years
<u>Science-</u>	3 years
<u>Social Studies-</u> (U.S. history and government;	
geography):	3 years
<u>Foreign language-</u>	2 years

- Let your child pursue his/her passion in electives: College look for a well rounded high school experience. Encourage your child to pursue his/her interest in art, music, journalism, computer programming, business, or performing arts.

- Help your child show what he/she Knows:
Many colleges require SAT. Subject Test scores for admission or placement. Your child can choose from 20 one-hour SAT subject Tests (formerly SAT II; Subject Test).

- Talk to your child's School Counselor early and often: The Counsellor or College adviser is a great resource for College Planning.

- Why the SAT? It's no secret that different high schools around the country have different courses and different grading standards.

- That's where the SAT comes in; it provides a common yardstick by which colleges can measure student's readiness for college-level work. The SAT measures students reasoning and critical thinking skills by asking them to apply what they have learned in high school.
    o   The SAT is NOT an intelligence test
    o   The SAT is NOT an achievement test
    o   The SAT is NOT the only deciding factor in College admissions

The high school transcript-evaluated by both the rigor of the courses and by the grades, is the most important factor in any admission decision. Along with application essays, extracurricular activities, and recommendation from teachers and counsellors, the SAT helps colleges and students arrive at the best fit.

AN OVERVIEW of the SAT

The SAT lasts 3 hours and 45 minutes and measures the core reasoning abilities students need to do college level work successfully.

Here's an overview of the SAT's Section and question types:

- The Writing Section: 60 minutes. Students write a short essay and answer multiple choice questions that test how well they use standard writing English.

- The Critical Reading Section: 70 minutes: This section includes reading passages with related questions and sentences completions that test critical reading.

Free Preparation Resources from the College Board

At www.collegeboard.com, the SAT Preparation Center offers test direction, practice questions, and a full length practice test. The SAT question of the day is a popular online feature that helps students familiarize themselves with question formats. The SAT Preparation Booklet gives test directions, practice questions, plus a practice test. It is available free at www.collegeboard.com and through your school.

Additional College Board Resources

The Official SAT Study Guide contains 8 actual practices test, and the official SAT Online Course is interactive, personalized, comprehensive and available anytime and anywhere. These can be purchased online at www.collegeboard.com

Financial Planning – College can be affordable - whatever your family's income; wherever you live; whatever your background.

Sources of financial support are available for every student, in every situation. In fact, 105 billion was available to students and their family in 2003! So get informed, get prepared, and get your share of the financial support you need.

Where's the Money?

There are three kinds of financial aid, all intended to fill the gap between what college cost and what your family can afford to pay.

- Grants and Scholarships: People call this "gift aid" because it doesn't have to be paid back. Grants and scholarships can be based on need or merit.

- Work Study: This is a federal program in which students work 10 to 20 hours per week to help pay education expenses.

- Parent/student loans: Most financial aid is in the form of low interest loans with no repayment or interest required until after graduation.

Applying for Financial Aid

Are you eligible for federal financial aid programs? To find out complete the FAFSA(Free Application for Federal Students Aid) Produced and processed by the U.S Department of Education it is available as a paper application or on the web at www.fafsa.ed.gov.

Many institution also ask students to complete the CSS/Financial AID Profile (available on our website under Student Tools) or their own application in order to apply for their financial aid program. Be sure to ask each college which applications are required.

Finding Scholarship

Here are some quick tips to get you started looking for scholarships:

A. Think Local-Check with your school Counsellor.

B. Think Big- Consider the large national scholarship funds, including Reserve Officer Training Corps(ROTC, Millennium, Coca-cola, And Robert Byrd).

C. Think Membership- See if your union, religious Organization or community or fraternal organization offers scholarships to children of members.

D. Think Employer- Many large companies offer scholar-ships or tuition reimbursement program for dependent children of employees. Check your human resources department.

E. Think College- College distribute a lot of scholarships . Find out what's available at the colleges your child may be exploring.

F. Think Ahead! Visit : www.collegeboard.com and Check out our free Scholarship search tool under the "For Student" heading. The College Board Scholarship Handbook is available at the Colleges Board online store.

Choosing a College: The choice can seem overwhelming, but don't panic: There are a lot of schools out there, and chances are that more than one is the "right" choice for your child. Three basic step can guide the search process:

Step 1 – An Honest Assessment- You child needs to think about his own personal interests, goals, personality traits, social considerations, extracurricular activities, and appropriate school size and location. While you should be prepared with a list of your own hopes and expectation for your child, be prepared to listen and be flexible.

Step 2: College Research- Before starting, be sure you and your child know the variety of college option available from liberal arts colleges to universities from technical and professional schools to community colleges, and from historical black colleges and universities to women's colleges.

- Use the high school counselling office: Ask about college fairs and student-parent nights.

- Talk to people: Encourage your child to talk to friends, family members anyone who's gone to college.

- Go to the internet: Visit: www.college.board.com and use the college search engine. Other sites include: www.campustours.com and www.colleges.possible.org

A Parent's Role

College application time is often anxiety-filled- for students and their parents. Here are some suggestions to help:

- <u>Get organized</u>- Suggest that your child dedicate a folder to each college with a checklist of required materials and their due dates.

- <u>Brain storm together</u> – Ask your child about the activities and awards that he/she is most proud of, any why they matter. Make a list to help highlight special strengths.

- Gather Key Information: Be sure your child know her Social Security number and high school code. Talk to the counsellor to make sure the high school transcript will be sent to the colleges on your child list.

- Get letters of recommendation: Recommendations can create a fuller picture of your child. Aim for small number of letters by people who can write about your child with some depth.

- Apply online: 225 Colleges and universities use a common application form, available online at: www.commonapp.org. Also, your child can apply online to hundred of schools through the College Board Website.

Winter- Encourage your parents to complete income tax forms early. If your parents have not completed their tax form. You can provide estimated information on your federal Student Aid application to make any necessary changes later.

If you have any question, about the federal student aid program or need assistance with the application process: call 1-800-4-FED-AID (1-800-433-3243) or the TTY for the hearing impaired, 1-800-730-8913

- After you submit the FAFSA, you should receive your Student Aid Report (SAR) within one to three weeks. Quickly make any necessary correction and submit them to the FAFSA processor.

- Complete Scholarship Application

Spring
Visit Colleges that have invited you to enrol.

- Review your college acceptance and compare financial aid package.

This was the story of Christopher Gray; a high school junior growing up in Birmingham, Alabama. Christ Knew he wanted to achieve opportunities beyond his circumstances and with his mother unemployed, he knew that it would be a tough road ahead.

Chris saw college as a necessity priced like a luxury good, so he began the tedious process on Scholly received the nations attention and adoration when it was featured on "Shark Tank", landing a deal with "Daymond John," and "Lori Greiner" while sparks the biggest fight in "Shark Tank" history. Shortly thereafter, Scholly grew to be the #1 overall app in both the IOS APP Store and the Google Play Store for over a while.

The company was named in Inc. Magazines Top College Start Ups, won under Armour's Cupid's Cup Competition and won Steve Case's Rise of the Rest Competition.

Chris Gray was named Ernst and Young's Entrepreneur of the Year for 2015 for Philadelphia and is one of Forbes '30 under 30 for 2016. Scholly has also been featured in just about every major media outlet, including. Good Morning America, Forbes BET, USA Today, Fortune Magazine, Smithsonian Magazine CNN, FOX News, and many more.

Chris won over $ 1.3 million in scholarships, including scholarship from the Bill and Melinda Gates Foundation and the Coca-Cola Scholar's Foundation, and was able to study finance and entrepreneurship a Drexel University in Philadephia. He was even able to cover his living expenses for all four years.

He learned how to find, apply for, and win scholarships, and became an expert on the broken state of the current scholarship ecosystem.

Most import to the Scholly team are the hundreds of thousands of students and families who have been able to use the platform to find over $ 70 million in scholarship money to go to college of their dream : To apply

Go To: Scholly-Scholarship Search Tool and College Scholarship Finder App.

If you haven't done so already, register for and take exam such as the SAT 1, SAT II; Subject Test or ACT for college admission. Check with the colleges you are interested in to see what test they require.

- Apply to the college you have chosen. Prepare your application carefully. Follow the instructions and pay close Attention To Deadline.

12 grade Cores

English
Math (Trigometry or Calculus)
Social Studies (Word Cultural, Geography or Any Social Studies, elective)

Graduation Requirement By State

VA: 22

Alabama: 24

Alaska: 21

Indiana: 20

New York: 22

N.C.: 20

Ohio : 20

CAL: 13

State does not offer technical diploma option but does provide a Certificate of Completion.

12 GRADE ALL YEAR

- Keep taking classes that challenge you.

- Work hard all year, second-semester grades can affect scholarship eligibility.

- Stay involved and seek leadership roles in your activities.

- <u>Fall</u>- Meet with your school counsellor to make sure you are on track to graduate and fulfil College admission requirements.

- If you haven't done so already, register for and take exams such as SAT1, SAT II ; Subject Test or ACT for College admission, Check with the colleges you are interest in to see what test they require.

- Apply to the college you have chosen. Prepare your application carefully, follow the instructions and Pay Close Attention To Deadlines!

- Well before your application deadlines, ask your counsellor and teaches to submit required documents (e.g.. transcript, letter of recommendation) to the college to which you're applying.

- To prepare to apply for federal student aid, be sure to get PIN at www.pin.ed.gov so that you can complete your application and access your information online. One of your parents must also get a PIN.

- **Winter-** Encourage your parents to complete income tax forms early. If your parents have not completed their tax forms, you can provide estimated information on your federal student aid application to make any necessary changes later.

- As soon after January 1 as possible, complete and submit your free application for Federal student Aid (FAFSA) a long with any other financial Aid application your school of choice may require you can complete the FAFSA online at.

- Contact a school's financial aid office if you have question about the aid that school has offered you. In fact, getting to know your financial aid staff early is a good idea no matter what. They can tell you about deadlines, other aid for which you can apply, and important paperwork you might need to submit.

- When you decide which school you want to attend, notify that school of your Commitment and submit any required financial deposit. Many schools require this notification and deposit by May 1.

* This checklist is available in PDF at: www.studenta;d.ed.gov/collprep.

CHAPTER 3

DONE ON MY END

Darcell & Dad
Add their part

First To Receive Scholarship from
Program "Vision" Going to the next Level

1. Plan in Place and he wanted to go to a D1 program, Mr. Whitaker started <u>putting his plan with checklist !!!</u>

    a. Pre High School
    b. High School- Every year
    c. 10th Grade
    d. 11th Grade
    e. 12th Grade

- <u>Fall</u> – Take the Preliminary SAT-National
- <u>Spring</u> – Register for and take exams for College Admission
- Summer Before 12th grade

Remember: Register for all tests in advance and be sure to give yourself time to prepare appropriately if you have difficulty paying a registration fee, see your school counsellor about getting a fee waiver.

This program Vision: Going to the Next Level, is designed to help the reader/ student hone the vision, create, improve, and execute the academic plan and necessary steps that takes the vision from a simple longing and desire all the way to reality.

<u>Definition</u> – <u>Vision</u>: Ability to see; sight or eyesight; something that you imagine a picture that you see in your mind. Something that you see or dream especially as part of a religious or supernatural experience.

Vision: Going to the Next Level (Duties)
<u>Steps to Take</u>

- Everything is based around first understanding that a plan for success exists, then preparing the said plan, and finally presenting it. Granted many students get scholarship, but they don't have the GPA (Grade point average) nor then have SAT, and ACT scores to reach the next level.

- Rather than going through Clearing House, I can show students, how to reach this next level for a scholarship in music, sports, drama, cheerleaders, and a myriad of other endeavours, say Revish.

- One student who followed the manual received a four year scholarship to the acclaimed Norfolk State University in Aug. 2012

- This student received his B.S. in History May 2016 from Norfolk State University.

- This student transferred to Virginia State University to work toward his Masters August 2016.

- December 2018, this student completed his Masters, and got accepted to work toward his PHD.

- Completed one year working toward P.H.D.

- Drop out P.H.D. program due to Virus and open up Group Home.

First D1 Offer

PETERSBURG FOOTBALL NEWS

Petersburg senior offensive tackle Darcell Whitaker (64) talks strategy with one of the Petersburg assistant coaches on Friday. Whitaker will play football next fall at Hampton.

Hampton Bound

Whitaker to play Division I college football

BY COURT WILLS
SPORTS WRITER

PETERSBURG — For some athletes, winning can be used as motivation.

But for Petersburg senior offensive tackle Darcell Whitaker, his driving motivation is his grandmother.

"She is my motivation. When I don't feel like practicing or running drills I think of her. She's a fighter," Whitaker said.

Over the past year, Whitaker's grandmother has been battling leukemia and because of the strength and positivity she has shown, the senior wants to fight even harder.

Because of that fight and that will to succeed, Whitaker

Homecoming pep rally that he has accepted a scholarship to play Division I college football next fall at Hampton University.

"I'm very excited because I wanted to make her proud. I felt like that Hampton was a good fit for me," Whitaker said. "They say that they will probably use me as an offensive tackle but will give me a shot to play offensive guard."

For four years, Whitaker has played diligently and improved each year under Petersburg football coach Mike Scott.

"He is the most improved player that I've had over these four years. He has improved his academics, his footwork, his quickness and his overall study of the game," Scott said. "He has a tough work ethic."

The 6-4, 330 pound offensive tackle had been offered by Norfolk State, but decided to go to Hampton where other Petersburg football players have gone

being Kendall Langford who is now playing for the Miami Dolphins.

"I always wanted to play college football I just didn't know where. The first college football game that I saw was a Florida-Florida State game and after that I wanted to play for the Florida Gators," Whitaker said.

But even though, Whitaker will not be attending Florida, he is proud about becoming a Hampton Pirate next fall.

"I just loved the family type of atmosphere. There is a lot of prestige that goes with going to Hampton with its academic background," Whitaker said. "And with Kendall Langford and Jerome Mathis having gone there that's even better. I am glad that I get to carry on that Petersburg pride with me."

Over his four-year career at Petersburg, one of the b[...]

Home News Forums Football FB Recruiting
Basketball BB Recruiting Baseball Girls BBall More

May 20, 2011
First offer in for Petersburg lineman
Rod Johnson
VirginiaPreps.com. Senior Editor

Related Links:
Class of 2012 prospects
V.I.P. Messageboard
VirginiaPreps.com Video
Vault

Talk about it in V. I. P. -
'MEMBERS ONLY' CLUB

In a deep class of offensive lineman in the state of Virginia from the Class of 2012, Petersburg High School's Darcell Whitaker ranks among the biggest in the state as rising senior stands 6-foot-5 and weighs in at 286 pounds. Despite his college-ready size, Whiteaker is currently only 16 years old meaning that a growth spurt may still be in cards for the Crimson Wave's big man.

After missing his sophomore season, Whitaker may have slipped a bit under the radar but his situation is rapidly changing as colleges visit the Wave program.

Norfolk State University recently became the first school to offer Whitaker as the Spartans threw their hat into the ring for the Central Region lineman's services though he is on the radar of several other schools as he claims to be interested in Arizona State, Duke, East Carolina, Georgia Tech, Hampton, USC, Marshall, San Jose State and Temple adding that both Notre Dame and Pitt have contacted him recently.

"I'm still wide open to hear from anyone," says Whitaker. "My main focus is in the classroom and helping lead my team to a state championship and my family."

With the first offer in his pocket, the rising senior is not going to rest on his laurels.

"I'm just working to improve as a person and athlete and trying to become the best that God will allow me to be."

A physical player with long arm and good hands, Whitaker collected the MVP award for offensive lineman at the NUC event held in Richmond in April.

Graduation Photo from Petersburg High School

Darcell Whitaker
June 2012

Darcell Whitaker Story Getting To The Next Level. Go to: "youtube" darcell Whitaker, and Virginia preps.com/darcellwhitaker

Signing Contract For Norfolk State University

Norfolk State
Virginia State

Signing Contract
For Scholarship

Darcell Whitaker, with
Father: Roy Whitaker
Author of Vision: Going To The Next Level

by: Virgil Revish

Darcell Whitaker, watch his father Roy Whitaker Sign his part of the Scholarship

We all three Rejoying after the sign of the Scholarship

Letter Send to Schools
to get Recruited

Writing a Letter
(Keep it brief)

Name
Street Address
City, State, Zip Code
Date:

Dear Coach;

Allow me to introduce myself. I am   , presently a
student-athlete at located in   . I am
and am of   years of age. My primary position is   .
I also play   . I am a hard worker, a winner, and a unique
football player dedicated to becoming the Best Football Player and
Team Player that I can possible be. Off the field I plan to become a
role model and positive leader in our community.

I just want to inform you of my interest in your football program. If you would like to view some of my highlights. Please go
to youtube.com/   . I can be contacted at the above address,
or by email at

I am looking forward to hearing from you in the future.

Sincerely,

Morning before Graduation
PHS.

The NCAA Eligibility Center, formally known as the NCAA Eligibility Clearinghouse is where recruits will need to register and be cleared in order to participate in college sports, College sports program will be unable to offer Division 1 and Division II recruit athletes scholarships until they have registered with the NCAA Eligibility Center.

Each of the three NCAA division have separate NCAA eligibility rules in which potential recruits are required to meet. Student athletes need to decide which Division Level they will be best matched for in order to determine which NCAA eligibility Rules they will fall under.

Athletes who are serious about getting recruit will need to do more that just registering with the NCAA eligibility Center. Athletes need to keep in mind that registering with the eligibility Center is only necessary if they are planning to complete at the NCAA Division I or Division II Level.

College coaches need to know more about each individual athlete an athletic scholarship. Be sure to take the appropriate steps to get recruited, don't wait around for a coach to find you.

Division III – After you create you profile. Tell them the best way they can stay in touch with you as you complete high school.

Maintaining Eligibility

After being recruited, this is where your will here the term "Continuing eligibility" and "Process toward degree", which means that students need to stay on track in order to maintain progress toward a "Baccalaureate or Equivalent Degree to stay eligible to at the NCAA level.

The Program:

Vision: Going To The Next Level!!! Success!!!

Received 4 year Scholarship to Play at Norfolk State University

Darcell Whitaker

Height- 6'4"   Weight- 285 lbs
Class: Senior   Hometown- Petersburg.Va
School-Norfolk State University

Preparing Workout Before Game

Darcell Whitaker
After Game, Take family member in Locker Room.

Division I

In 2016, continued his education at Virginia State University, working, toward his Masters. December 2018, received his Masters from Virginia States University in Administration.

UPTON BAILEY SUCCESS

4

Second To Receive Scholarship From
Program "Vision" Going To The Next Level

How did Mr. Virgil Revish inspire me?
He showed me the right way to lead
and lead by example Mr. Revish also showed
me how to carry myself the right way
and right people. He also showed me the
business side of life.

Upton Bailey Success

UPTON BAILEY

I started working with Upton Bailey fall of 2018. I told his father that I was interested in working with his son, and get to the next level. The next evening, we sat down and talked about Upton's future. His father told me that Upton had been invited to participate in the Blue-Gray All American Bowl, Saturday, January 4, 2020, Tampa Bay Buccaneer's Raymond James Stadium at 1:30 p.m. , presented by Blue-Gray Events and ESPN3. Mr. Bailey said he didn't have the money to register him for the event. I asked him " How much to register him so he won't miss this opportunity. Mr. Bailey said$ 495.00 and Petersburg High School, covered the different. After everything was finalized for the Blue-Gray All American Bowl, Mr. Bailey drove down to the Blue-Gray All American Bowl with family members, and meet other family members that lived in the area when they arrived.

The day of the competition, after everything said and done, Upton Bailey come back to Virginia with the Most Valuable Trophy, and is from Petersburg High School, Petersburg, Virginia.

This is the Trophy Upton
Bailey brought back from the
Blue-Gray All American Bowl.

Most Valuable Trophy
from Blue-Gray All
<u>American Bowl</u>- Saturday,
January 4, 2020. Tampa Bay
Buccaneer's Raymond James Stadium
At 1:30 p.m.

Presented by- Blue-Gray Events and ESPN3

Interviewed By Ch. 6 Telling Ch. 6 News
What School He was Signing With

Supporting Upton Bailey At Ch. 6 Interview

Sitting With Family Members at Ch. 6 Interview

Senior Night

Upton Bailey also Played basketball as a Second sport for Petersburg High School.

This was Senior Night

Uptown Bailey, Zyshawn White, Meziah Scott all three played in the Spring Game 2023. Uptown Bailey scored on rushing and Zyshawn scored on receiving and Meziah Scott came in as quarterback and all three of them did well. #1 is Uptown Bailey #8 is Zyshawn White and #15 is Meziah Scott all three did well and all three went to Petersburg High School. Other gentleman is Uptown Bailey Senior

Upton Bailey and Zyshawn White, Both Played In The "Spring Game" and They Both Scored, Upton Bailey Running Back on The Left and Zyshawn White Receiver, Upton Bailey Scored on Rushing, and Zyshawn White Scored on Receiving. They Both Went To Petersburg High School, Petersburg, Virginia (send photo later)

Accomplishments of The Program Vision: Going To The Next Level

5

Petersburg Public School Member
Accomplishments of the Program:
"Vision": Going To The Next Level-1999.

Mr. Virgil Revist School Watch

PPS TEAM MEMBER

THANKS!

OUR PPS SPED TEAM IS SUCCESSFUL BECAUSE
OF YOUR
OUTSTANDING
SUPPORT, COOPERATION, AND
PROFESSIONALISM
I AM CONFIDENT ABOUT THE FUTURE FOR OUR
STUDENTS
BECAUSE OF YOUR PROVEN COMMITMENT TO
MAKING
OPUR WORLD
A
BETTER PLACE
HAVE A MERRY CHRISTMAS
AND
A
HAPPY Y2K!!!
PEACE, LOVE, AND HAPPINESS!
LARRY J. BROWN, SR.
12/17/99

2014

Proof the "Vision "System Really Works!

Vision: Celebrated College Prep Manual Prepares to Mark Reader's Graduation from University-Proof the 'Vision' System Really Works!

In 2014, Virgil Revish rocked the college prep manual world with the release of 'Vision' – Going to the Next Level', designed to help young readers reach the destiny they dream of through a structured and logical program. One of the first readers was Darcell Whitaker, who is about to graduate from Norfolk State and continue his education at VSU on another football scholarship. It's all thanks to Revish and his unique creation, and family members.

For Immediate Release

South Chesterfield, VA –in 2014 media across the United States met Darcell Whitaker, who was enjoying a four year football scholarship to Norfolk State University thanks to his utilization of the market's newest and most unconventional college prep guide, 'Vision-Going to the next level'.

The great news is that Whitaker is about to graduate, and continue his football career @ some University this fall while studying for his masters. And guess what? It's all due to his continued participation in the 'Vision' program.

The program is the brainchild of Vigil Revish, and available to anyone in definitive book form.

Synopsis:

In all phases and stages of life, there are many options, opportunities and paths that one can take. Usually, however, there is a process, that may have many roads that will lead an individual to success.

The purpose of this Manual is to identify and define some of the roads, opportunities and options and to help the reader, through a planned program, to reach his/her destiny.

Without regard for the individual, everyone seeking success needs a VISION and a plan. This manual, VISION- Going to the Next level is more than a plan.

It is program designed to help the reader/student hone the vision, create, improve and execute the academic plan and necessary steps that takes the Vision from a simple longing and desire all the way to reality.

Let's get started now to define your Vision and understand as you prepare to take the steps that will lead to your success.

"Darcell has done so well because, from day one, he had a plan," explains Revish. "This plan is exactly what the Vision system sets out to foster and, because he followed it, his football career and education are continuing at no cost to him. It's proof that my system really works and that it's paint-by-numbers format could mean the difference between young people not going to college and going on a free ticket to success!"

Revish breaks his program down into a series of simple steps, each followed by Darcell to the letter:

1. Improved overall academic performance and improved grade point averages (GPA) by changing study habits
2. Working consistently with a teacher in the area in which students are having problems
3. Conditioning the body to be physically prepared to cope with the strains of intense studying
4. Scheduling regular workouts which, for Darcell, were with his high football team
5. Incorporating an off-season workout plan

"I won't lie and say that Darcell has it easy; his success has taken blood, sweat and tears, but now he has a competitive advantage over all of his peers. Anyone can replicate his success- just pick up a copy of the book!" Revish adds.

'Vision: Going to the Next Level' is available now Amazon, Barnes-N-Nobels

For more information, visit the author's official website: http:www.virgilrevish.com.

Speaking Engagement Contact: (804) 835-9434

About the Author:

In 2014, Virgil Revish rocked the college prep manual world with the release of "Vision" Going To The Next Level', designed to help young reach the destiny they dream of through a structured and logical program. One of the first readers was Darcell Whitaker who graduated from Norfolk State University, May 2016 with B. S. in "History", and continued his education at Virginia August 2016, and December 2018 received his "Masters" in "Administration". January 2019 got excepted to work toward his P.H.D.. Completed one year toward his P.H.D. , then the "Virus" hit the world. Darcell Whitaker dropped out of school, and open up a "Group Home" 2020.

Virgil C. Revish is an author, consultant, motivational speaker, and mentor. He taught at junior high until he joined the U.S. Army and served for 3 to 5 years. Due to his devotion to students and education, he returned to teaching. He taught in Fairfax, VA for four years. He Later worked at Petersburg wastewater treatment plant, testing water samples and reading meters. From September 1993 to June 1999, he started a volunteer program called " School Watch" in sex Petersburg schools. In 2000 he worked in an after school program called Achievers plus at the Children's Home of Virginia Baptist.

Contact:

Virgil Revish

virgilrevish@yahoo.com

Cell - 804-735-3431

Linkedin/Virgil Revish

In 2014, The White House
Washington, D.C. July 1, 2014

Appreciate, me sharing my story of the young man who was the first leader to receive a four year scholarship from the program: Vision: Going To The Next Level.

THE WHITE HOUSE

WASHINGTON

July 1, 2014

Mr. Virgil Revish
South Chesterfield, Virginia

Dear Virgil:

Thank you for writing. I have heard many personal accounts from individuals and families across our country, and I appreciate your sharing your story with me.

Each day, I read letters from Americans so that I stay connected to their real-life and diverse experiences. By working together and involving all Americans in shaping the policies that affect us, we will build a brighter future for ourselves and our Nation.

Thank you, again, for sharing your story. I wish you all the best for the future.

Sincerely,

In 2016 – Student Achieve Prestigious Scholarship

Vision: Life-Changing New College Prep Manual Empowers Students to Reach 'Next Level', With Readers Already achieving Prestigious Scholarships.

Concieved and constructed by Virgil Revish, 'Going to the Next Level' is unlike any other college prep manual ever written. With a model that includes students acknowledging a plan, preparing their plan and then presenting it, Revish is making scholarships available to those who would traditionally find them out of reach. One reader, Darcell Whittaker, has already won a four-year scholarship Virginia's Norfolk State University.

For Immediate Release

South Chesterfield, VA- While hundreds of college prep guides exist on the market, most fail to give students a concrete plan for success. Stepping in to not only give young people the plan they need, but increase their chances of winning a prestigious college scholarship, Virgil Revish is delighted to announce the launch of his new book.

'Vision: Going to the Next Level' is revolutionary to say the least. Based around three steps to a student's 'plan', the soon-to-be-released resource is already seeing amazing success in the field.

Synopsis:

In all phases and stages of life, there are many options, opportunities and paths that one can take. Usually, however, there is a process, that may have many roads that will lead an individual to success.

The purpose of thus Manual is to identify and define some of the roads, opportunities and options and to help the reader, through a planned program, to reach his/her destiny.

Without regard for the individual, everyone seeking success needs a VISION and a plan. This manual, VISION-Going to the Next Level is more than a plan.

It is program designed to help the reader/student hone the vision, create, improve and execute the academic plan and necessary steps that takes the Vision from a simple longing and desire all the way to reality.

ħ I would like to discuss about continuing education and getting to the next level. I am focusing on Middle and High school after activities, churches, college, etc.

ħ The things that I want to discuss with each group is the test of that person or people whether they will recognize it and respond in obedience to the one who is offering it, trusting his ability to work, to refrain for the opportunity that God has for you.

ħ   The reason who I am an expert is Vision: Life changing college prep manual empowers students to Reach next level with readers already achieving prestigious scholarships and Vision: Celebrates College Prep manual prepares to mark Reader's Graduation from university. Proof the Vision system really works

We had one reader that has already won a four year scholarship for Norfolk State University.

When the time is available, I would like to have lunch and discuss with you the educational opportunities

In 2016-The White House

Mr. President Obama said our Nation has made great Strides over the last 7 years, and we should be proud of what we have accomplished together.

THE WHITE HOUSE

WASHINGTON

July 21, 2016

Mr. Virgil Revish
South Chesterfield, Virginia

Dear Virgil:

Thank you for writing. Our Nation has made great strides over the last 7 years, and we should be proud of what we have accomplished together. I'm humbled by the privilege to serve in this Office, but I suspect that more than my Presidency, it's the optimism, and hard work of people like you that have changed our country for the better.

America still faces many challenges, and our success is not inevitable. It will depend on all people raising their voices, rejecting the cynical notion that progress is not possible, and making sure our politics reflect what is best in us. I will keep your words of support in mind as I continue doing all I can help bring about the kind of lasting change we can only make together.

Sincerely,

NFL player giving back

Pictured together are NFL Player Quinton Spain, instructors, volunteers and several of the 186 young men who attended the first Quinton Spain Football Camp held at Petersburg High School on Saturday, June 25, 2016. PHOTOS BY NICHOLAS VANDELOECHT/PROGRESS-INDEX.COM

Tennessee Titans lineman Spain holds football camp for area youth

In 2019, I Participated in the nation largest Reading celebration, and received a Reader Across America Day Certificate of Appreciation

2016

Quinton Spain Stats, Height, Weight, Position, Draft, College

Quenton Lamar Spain is an American football guard who is currently a free agent. He was signed by the Tennessee Titans as an undrafted free agent in 2015. He played College football at West Virginia

Born: 1991 (age 31 years), Petersburg, Va.
Number: 67 (Cincin Bengal/Guard)
Position: Offensive lineman, Guard
Education: Petersburg High School, West Virginia University
Weight: 335 llb.

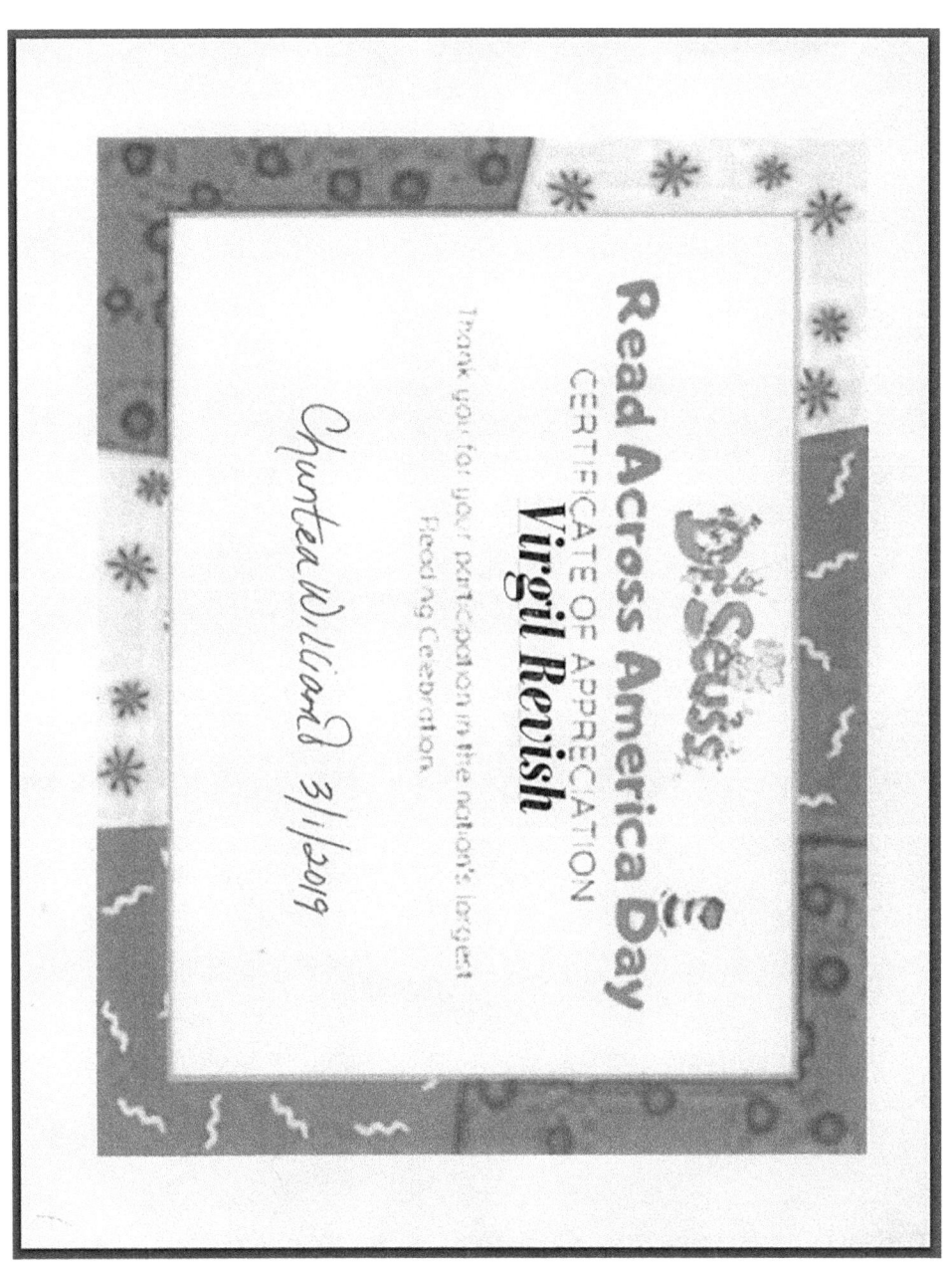

Press Release

2021 City's Best

<u>Award Winner!!</u>

Press Release (2021)

PRESS RELEASE

FOR IMMEDIATE RELEASE

Virgil Revish Wins City's Best Award

The City's Best Awards judging panel honoured Virgil Revish with the 2021 City's Best Award based on their outstanding service and customer satisfaction over the last year.

Competition for the award was high due to the businesses opening in the area, despite the downturn recently in commerce due to the pandemic. Several businesses stood out from the crowd, but Virgil Revish came out on top.

Partnering with only the best businesses., The City's Best Awards works with one winner in each major city throughout pthe country. This winner is selected annually and receives various perks including an exclusive business listing, a website badge, award certificate, social media graphics, and more.

The City's Best Awards wishes the best for Virgil Revish in the 2021-2022 season and sincere congratulations on their winning of his prestigious award.

###

CITY'S BEST AWARDS WINNER

Congratulations to

VIRGIL REVISH

for being selected as the award recipient
for the 2021 City's Best Award.

CERTIFICATE
OF APPRECIATION

THE FOLLOWING AWARD IS GIVEN TO

Virgil C. Revish

on behalf of Blandford 6th Grade Academy for your generous donations to our school. We truly appreciate your generosity and support!

Trina Mitchener

Trina Mitchener
Associate Princiapal

Padraic Hampton

Padraic Hampton
Assistant Principal

Communities
in Schools
Petersburg

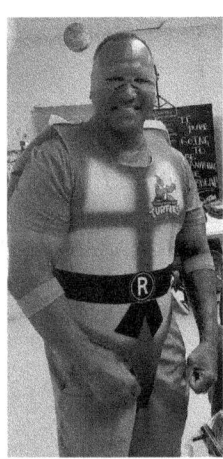

One of our "School Board" member, visiting classroom for "Fall Festivity"(Mr. Hal Miles) pg.101, Associate Principal (Trina Mitchener, and Assistance Principal (Padraic Hampton) visiting classrooms for Festivity.

www.ingramcontent.com/pod-product-compliance
Lightning Source LLC
Chambersburg PA
CBHW051225120626
46547CB00013B/1517